Life of Fred™

Butterflies

Life of Fred™
Butterflies

Stanley F. Schmidt, Ph.D.

Polka Dot Publishing

ISBN: 978-0-9791072-5-2

Library of Congress Catalog Number: 2011924327
Printed and bound in the United States of America

Polka Dot Publishing   Reno, Nevada

To order copies of books in the Life of Fred series,

visit our website PolkaDotPublishing.com

Questions or comments? Email Polka Dot Publishing at lifeoffred@yahoo.com

Third printing

Life of Fred: Butterflies was illustrated by the author with additional clip art furnished under
license from Nova Development Corporation, which holds the copyright to that art.

for Goodness' sake

or as J.S. Bach—who was
never noted for his plain
English—often expressed it:

Ad Majorem Dei Gloriam
(to the greater glory of God)

If you happen to spot an error that the author, the publisher, and the printer missed, please let us know with an email to: lifeoffred@yahoo.com

As a reward, we'll email back to you a list of all the corrections that readers have reported.

A Note Before We Begin
the Second Book in the Series

We all have dreams for our children. So quickly they grow up.

We would like them to have more than we had when we were young. Medicine is better nowadays. Dentistry is better.

Boy looking at toys.
Taken by G. G. Bain in
1910

Even toys have improved a little bit.

Choices for your children's math education have widened. In the old days, the math books all looked pretty much alike. A lesson would tell how to do something and then give 40 problems. Then the next lesson would tell how to do something else and give 40 more problems.

But they never really told why your child should learn the stuff.

Then came the colorful "new" math books. They were filled with photographs of jet airplanes and four-color diagrams. They were sometimes called coffee table math books: heavy, pretty, and expensive.

And each lesson would tell how to do something and give 40 problems. They were like the old math books except they wore lipstick.

Then came video math "education." Someone stood at a blackboard and read the lesson to the child. They were even more expensive than the coffee table math books.

Learning by video

Your child had even less experience in learning how to read. Since learning how to learn by reading is one of the most important skills for college and later life, video was a step in the wrong direction.

Each video lesson told how to do some piece of math and gave 40 problems to do.

And they never learned why they were supposed to learn the math.

In the old math books,
    in the coffee table math books,
        in the video,
            math was sealed off from the rest of the world. The pictures of jet airplanes or video of someone at the blackboard brought a predictable response from kids: "So what? Why am I learning this stuff?"

. . . and then there is Fred. All of life is wrapped up in the adventures of this five-year-old.
    In this book your child will learn reasons to count by fives,
                will learn how to set a table,
                    will learn about the giant star Betelgeuse, and
            a zillion other things.

Mathematics is taught in the *Life of Fred* series in the context of living a full life. A real education—not just memorizing math facts.

HOW THIS BOOK IS ORGANIZED

Each chapter is about six pages. Do a chapter a day.

At the end of each chapter is a Your Turn to Play.
Have a paper and pencil handy before you sit down to read.
Each Your Turn to Play consists of about four or five questions.
Have your child write out the answers.
After all the questions are answered, then take a peek at my answers that are given on the next page.

Don't just let your child read the questions and look at the answers.
Your child won't learn as much taking that shortcut.

CALCULATORS?

Not now. There will be plenty of time later (when students hit Pre-Algebra). Right now in arithmetic, our job is to learn the addition and multiplication facts by heart.

Contents

Chapter One
Kingie Dreams

Fred had pulled out a book about butterflies to read to his doll, Kingie. Fred sat in the corner and put Kingie on his lap. It was five o'clock in the afternoon.

Kingie was a doll that liked to draw and paint. He had been working all day on oil paintings.

5:00

With his little five-year-old voice, Fred was reading to Kingie about butterflies. There were pictures of all kinds of butterflies in the book.

When Fred was about halfway through the book, Kingie shut his eyes and fell asleep. Kingie was dreaming.

Fred usually sang to Kingie each night to help Kingie go to sleep. Since he was already asleep, Fred did not sing.

He picked Kingie up and carried him to the spot under his desk where they slept each night.

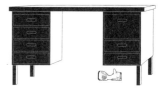

Fred wasn't sleepy yet. He put a bookmark in the butterfly book and put it back in its place on the shelf.

He turned out the light and headed out into the hallway outside his office. Fred is a teacher at KITTENS University. He and Kingie live in his office on the third floor of the math building.

There were nine vending machines in the hallway. Five of them were on one side, and four of them on the other side. Some were candy machines. One offered doughnuts. One offered crackers. One offered a soft drink called Sluice.

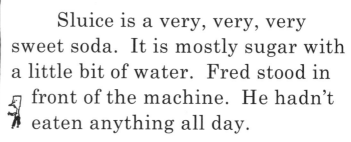

Sluice is a very, very, very sweet soda. It is mostly sugar with a little bit of water. Fred stood in front of the machine. He hadn't eaten anything all day.

14

He decided not to get a Sluice. It sometimes made him sick.

Fred did not have parents to watch over him.* No one had ever told Fred about eating the right foods.

Fred was five years old, but he was only one yard tall. He was as tall as a yardstick. One yard is three feet.

----------------one yard --------------------

Because of his poor eating habits, Fred had not grown an inch in a long time.

Fred started to head down the stairs.

"Hi!" said Betty. She was coming up the stairs as Fred was heading down the stairs. "I was just going to your office to see you."

Betty was one of Fred's students at KITTENS. She was one of the first people to meet Fred when he came to the university to teach four years ago. She and her boyfriend, Alexander, have shared many adventures with Fred over the years.

---

* It's a sad story that is told in *Life of Fred: Calculus.* It may not be suitable for the prepubescent mind.

"Hi Betty," Fred answered. "I was just going outside to get some fresh air. Kingie has been doing oil painting all day in my office. The room smells a bit like oil paint."

Betty said, "That sounds like a good idea. May I join you?"

When they got outside, Fred asked Betty why she had come to see him.

She was about to tell him about a calculus problem* that she was working on, when she looked up at the building.

"What's that coming out of your window!" Betty exclaimed. "It looks like little pieces of colored paper."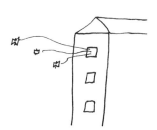

Fred could see better than Betty since his eyes were only five years

---

*

She had been trying to solve $\int \dfrac{1}{x^3 + 1}\, dx$ which is a problem from calculus.

The big long S $\int$ means "find the area under the curve."

It all looks very mysterious right now, but once you have studied arithmetic, algebra, geometry, and trig, learning how to find the area under $\dfrac{1}{x^3 + 1}$ will be no harder than what you are doing right now, which is learning about the numbers that add to 9.

old. He said, "No, that is not colored paper.
Those are butterflies."

Betty counted nine butterflies that came
out of Fred's window. Five of them landed on
the flowers. The other four landed
on Fred's head.

They tickled Fred.

Please take out a piece of
paper and write your answers.
After you are all done, you can check your work
on the next page.

Your Turn to Play

1. 5 + 4 = ?
2. 4 + 5 = ?
3. What time is it?

4. Fred is one yard tall. How many feet is that? (If
you have forgotten, it is okay to look back two pages to
find the answer.)

5. How many members does the set {1, 2, 3, 4, 5, 6}
have? (This was in *Life of Fred: Apples*.)

6. 2 + 5 = ? (This was also in *Apples*.)

.......ANSWERS.......

1. $5 + 4 = 9$
2. $4 + 5 = 9$
3. 5 o'clock or 5:00

4. One yard is three feet.
5. The set {1, 2, 3, 4, 5, 6} has six members in it.

Here are some other sets with six members:

{A, B, C, D, E, F}

{✳, ✤, ✿, ✾, ❀, ✺}

{●, ○, ■, ◆, ❖, ◗}

and the set of the days of the week that don't have an *h* in their spelling: {Sunday, Monday, Tuesday, Wednesday, Friday, Saturday}.

6. $2 + 5 = 7$

In *Apples* we did all the numbers that add to 7:

$$0 + 7 = 7$$
$$1 + 6 = 7$$
$$2 + 5 = 7$$
$$3 + 4 = 7$$
$$4 + 3 = 7$$
$$5 + 2 = 7$$
$$6 + 1 = 7$$
$$7 + 0 = 7$$

Chapter Two
Drawing Butterflies

The butterflies tickled Fred's head. He giggled, and the butterflies all flew away. The four butterflies joined the five that were on the flowers.

Betty and Fred sat very quietly on a bench to watch those nine butterflies.

Betty took out a piece of paper and drew one of the butterflies.

She gave Fred a piece of paper so that he could also draw.

Betty looked at Fred's drawing and smiled. She said, "I don't think their feet look like that."

Fred got another sheet of paper and drew a new picture.

Fred thought that this picture was much better. Now the butterfly had shoes on.

Betty had forgotten about asking about the calculus problem $\int \frac{1}{x^3 + 1} \, dx$. Instead, she asked, "How did those nine butterflies fly out of your office window?"

Fred said, "I left the window open."

Fred's answer was true, but it was not what Betty was really asking. She tried again: "I mean how did those butterflies get into your office in the first place?"

Fred wasn't sure. He answered, "I guess they flew in."

"But this is February in Kansas," Betty said. "This morning it was −15 degrees, and when it is 15 degrees below zero, you don't have butterflies flying around."

They decided to go back to his office and find out what was going on.

Fred climbed the steps one-at-a-time:

1 2 3 4 5 6 7 8 9 10 11 12 13 14 15 16

Betty's legs were a lot longer than Fred's. She took the stairs two-at-a-time:

2 4 6 8 10 12 14 16

When Fred was climbing the stairs, he tried to think of where the butterflies had come from.

He had been reading a book about butterflies to Kingie. Did the butterflies in the book come alive and fly out the window? No, that would be silly.

Kingie had been dreaming about butterflies. Did his dream break open and the butterflies fly out the window?

No. That would also be silly.

When they got to Fred's office, he told Betty that Kingie was sleeping. He said that they should be quiet so they wouldn't wake him up.

He carefully opened his office door. When he looked in, he got a surprise. Kingie was

awake and sitting on top of Fred's desk.

"What happened?" Fred asked.

Now, as everyone knows, when dolls talk, sometimes only their owners can hear them. So when Kingie told Fred what was happening, Betty didn't hear anything Kingie said.

Kingie told Fred, "First of all, I didn't go to sleep for the whole night. It is only ten minutes after five o'clock right now.

5:10

"Second, you forgot to sing to me, so I knew it wasn't time for my nighttime sleep.

"Third, what are those bugs on the top of your desk?"

Fred ran over to his desk to look.

He couldn't see any bugs on the top of his desk.

Please write your answers on a piece of paper before you look at my answers on the next page.

Your Turn to Play

1. Why couldn't Fred see the bugs?

2. Kingie started his nap at

5:00

He ended his nap at

5:10

How long had Kingie slept?

3. Betty went up the stairs two at a time.

2, 4, 6, 8, 10, 12, 14, 16. Continue this series up to 40. Your answer will look like: 2, 4, 6, 8, 10, 12, 14, 16, *18*, *20, 22*. . . .

4. Here is the set of days of the week that have an *s* in their names: {Sunday, Tuesday, Wednesday, Thursday, Saturday.} Write the set of the days of the week that have an *h* in their names.

. . . . **ANSWERS** . . . .

1. I think Fred couldn't see the bugs since he was too short to see the top of his desk.

That's not the only possible answer.

Some people might have written that Fred couldn't see the bugs because Kingie was standing in the way.

Some people might have written that Fred couldn't see the bugs because those things on the top of his desk were not bugs. They were pieces of string.

Moral: There is not always just one right answer to a question.

2. If Kingie started his nap at 5:00 and slept for 1 minute, he would have woken up at 5:01.

If he started at 5:00 and slept for 2 minutes, he would have woken up at 5:02.

If he started at 5:00 and slept for 3 minutes, he would have woken up at 5:03.

If he started at 5:00 and slept for 4 minutes, he would have woken up at 5:04.

If he started at 5:00 and slept for 5 minutes, he would have woken up at 5:05.

If he started at 5:00 and slept for 6 minutes, he would have woken up at 5:06.

If he started at 5:00 and slept for 7 minutes, he would have woken up at 5:07.

If he started at 5:00 and slept for 8 minutes, he would have woken up at 5:08.

If he started at 5:00 and slept for 9 minutes, he would have woken up at 5:09.

If he started at 5:00 and slept for 10 minutes, he would have woken up at 5:10.

3. 2, 4, 6, 8, 10, 12, 14, 16, *18, 20, 22, 24, 26, 28, 30, 32, 34, 36, 38, 40*

4. There is only one day of the week that has an *h* in its name. {Thursday}.

Chapter Three
A Bug Up Close

Fred piled a stack of books on the floor and stood on them. He moved Kingie so that he could see the bugs.

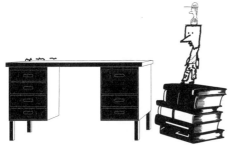

Kingie liked to sit on top of Fred's head. It was nice and flat.

The bugs were moving. They were crawling across the top of the desk. They were coming right toward Fred and Kingie.

Fred liked that. The closer they came, the better Fred could see them.

Kingie did not like that. He hopped off of Fred's head and ran over and stood next to Betty.

Fred leaned over. He wasn't afraid of bugs. He put his face right down on the desk top.

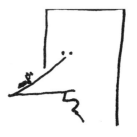

That might have been a mistake. One of the bugs crawled on his nose.

Kingie hid behind Betty's legs. He couldn't stand to watch Fred with a bug on his nose.

As the bug crawled on his nose, Fred could see what the bug really looked like:

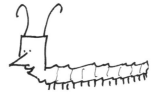

Time Out!

Sometimes things are too much. Sometimes things are too little.

Did you ever read the story of Goldilocks? One bowl of mush was too hot. One bowl was too cold. But the third bowl was just right.
One of the beds was too hard and the other was too soft. But the third one was just right.

Kingie was too afraid of bugs. He ran across the room and hid behind Betty.
Fred wasn't afraid enough. You shouldn't let bugs crawl on your nose.

Betty had just the right amount of fear. She picked the bug off of Fred's nose and put it back on the desk.

She explained to Fred: "Some bugs are nice and won't hurt you at all. Other bugs will bite!"

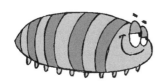 

(These two pictures are silly. Bugs do not have eyebrows.)

If you wanted to count the legs on the bug on the right, the hard way to do it would be to count all the left legs and then all the right legs: 1, 2, 3, 4, 5, 6, 7, 8.

It would be easier to count by twos: 2, 4, 6, 8.

"Are the bugs gone?" Kingie asked. He was still hiding behind Betty.

Betty told Kingie, "It's okay. These bugs are caterpillars. They don't bite people. Caterpillars just eat things like leaves."

Betty picked up Kingie and asked him, "Do you like butterflies?"

Kingie said, "Yes. They are pretty. It's those caterpillars that are ugly and scary."*

"Let me tell you a butterfly story," Betty said. She told Fred to draw pictures while she told the story.

Betty's story	Fred's pictures

Butterflies like to fly around.

> Error in Fred's drawing: Butterflies do not fly airplanes.

They lay eggs on leaves.

> Error in Fred's drawing: Butterflies do not lay eggs the size of chicken eggs. Butterfly eggs are small.

The eggs hatch and turn into caterpillars.

---

* And as everyone knows, sometimes when dolls talk, not just their owners can hear them.

The caterpillars eat a lot.
They grow up. They become a
chrysalis. (CHRIS–eh–lis)

Home Sweet
Cocoon

> Error in Fred's drawing:
> Moths use cocoons.
> Butterflies do not.

Butterflies hatch.
They spread their wings
and fly away to find a leaf
to lay their eggs on.

Your Turn to Play

1. How many eyes are on these caterpillars?

2. Starfish have five legs. How many legs on these starfish?
(It's much easier if you count by fives.)

3. This is the set of months beginning with *M*:
{March, May}.

    Write the set of months beginning with *F*.

4. $4 + 5 = ?$
5. $5 + 2 = ?$

. . . . ANSWERS . . . .

1.

    2   4   6   8   10   12   14   16

2.

    5   10   15   20   25   30

3. The set of months beginning with *F*: {February}.

When you list the members of a set, you always put them in braces.

                Braces   { }
                Parentheses   ( )
                Brackets   [ ]

4. $4 + 5 = 9$
5. $5 + 2 = 7$

Chapter Four
Putting Kingie to Bed

When Fred and Betty had been outside, they had seen nine butterflies fly out of Fred's office window. Now they knew where the butterflies had come from.

If there were caterpillars in his office, then some of them became chrysalises.

If some of them had become chrysalises, then after a while, they would have hatched into butterflies.

If there were butterflies in his office, then they would have flown out of his window to find leaves to lay their eggs on.

What if there had been 10 butterflies and 9 of them flew out the window to find leaves to lay their eggs on?

$$10 - 9 = 1$$

Could one butterfly have found something that looked like a leaf right there in Fred's office?

Betty carefully took the eggs off of Kingie's hat. She did not tell him what she was doing so he wouldn't be frightened.

Betty took the eggs and all the caterpillars and put them in a paper bag. She told Kingie that she and Fred were going to take the bag outside.

5:25

It was twenty-five minutes after 5. It was getting dark outside. (That happens in Kansas in February. During the summer it stays light until 8 or 9.)

"It's time for you to go to sleep," Fred told his doll. "It's dark outside. I have already read to you."

"But you haven't sung to me yet," Kingie said.*

Fred headed to the poetry section of his books and took down a book by one of his favorite poets: Christina Rossetti.

---

* Every doll has a different way of going to sleep at night.
　　Some want a story read to them.
　　　Some want to be sung to.
　　　　Some want a glass of water.
　　　　　Some want to practice their addition: $3 + 4 = 7$, $2 + 5 = 7$, $6 + 1 = 7$.
　　　　　Some just want to be held for a while.

He found one of his favorite poems, "Consider the Lilies. . . ." Fred put Kingie on his lap and made up the melody as he sang:

♪ But not alone the fairest flowers:
The merest grass   ♫
Along the roadside where we pass, . . . ♪
Tell of His love who sends the dew. . . .

Here is the sheet music for what Fred sang. If you can play the piano, you can sing along with Fred.

But Not Alone

Fred Gauss

Christina Rossetti's words were good.

Fred's singing sounded like most five-year-olds when they sing. But that was okay. Kingie loved it.

Kingie was soon asleep, and Fred put him back under his desk.

Fred turned out the light as he and Betty left the room. They passed the nine vending machines in the hallway—five on the right and four on the left.

They walked down the stairs and outside into the evening air. Betty opened the paper sack. She put the eggs and caterpillars on the leaves.

~~Betty tossed the paper bag on the ground.~~

She didn't do that. She is not a litterbug.

~~Betty ate the paper bag.~~

She didn't do that. She doesn't eat paper bags.

Betty put the paper bag in the garbage can. The students at KITTENS University are very proud of how nice their campus looks. There is no trash on the ground.

Betty asked, "Fred, have you had anything to eat today?" She knew that Fred often forgot to eat.

Fred thought for a moment. He remembered showing Kingie some pencils in the morning.

5 + 2 is 7

He remembered drawing a picture of a mouse.

He remembered going out jogging. About the big snow. About the deciduous roses. About Domenico Fetti's painting: *Archimedes Thoughtful.*

There was so much to remember. Finally, he told Betty that he couldn't remember eating today. He said, "We could go back into the math building, and I could get a Sluice."

Your Turn to Play

1. "A Sluice!" Betty exclaimed. "That's just sugar water! You are only a yard tall, and you are five years old!"

How many feet are in a yard?

2. How many exclamation points (!) are in the previous problem?

3. Count from 40 to 60 by twos.

4. Count from 40 to 60 by fives.

5. Do you think Betty is going to say yes to Fred's suggestion of getting a Sluice to drink?

· · · · · · · **ANSWERS** · · · · · · ·

1. There are three feet in a yard.

2. There are three exclamation points in question one. You use exclamation points to indicate surprise or excitement. Don't use them a lot!!!!!!! If you do, they start to lose their impact.

3. 40, 42, 44, 46, 48, 50, 52, 54, 56, 58, 60

4. 40, 45, 50, 55, 60

5. Betty was very excited in question one. (Three exclamation points.) Everything she said indicated that she thought Sluice would be a very bad idea for Fred.

Sugar does not help you grow. It just tastes good to many kids. Think of all the major kid "holidays": Halloween (candy), birthday parties (cake and ice cream), Christmas (candy canes), Easter (chocolate rabbits), and fast food places (Sluice and other sugar-filled soft drinks).

What kids' book ever mentions that sugar might be related to:

  ☹ getting fat

  ☹ having heart disease

  ☹ growing cancer cells

  ☹ hurting your immune system or

  ☹ becoming diabetic?

Many kids only know that sugar tastes good.

Chapter Five
At the Food Court

Betty explained to Fred that what he needed wasn't some sugar water. He should have some meat and some milk. The meat would give him protein. Protein is needed to grow muscles.

The milk would give him both protein and calcium. The calcium would help grow Fred's bones. She told him, "You can't grow tall if you have short bones."

She took Fred's hand, and they headed off to the food court on the KITTENS Campus. Almost all colleges have places to eat on campus. KITTENS was no exception.

In five minutes they were at the food court.

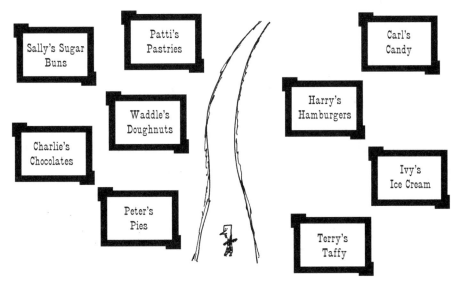

"It's just like the vending machines in the hallway outside my office," Fred said.

Betty thought he meant that so much of it was just sugar and white flour. But Fred was thinking mathematically.

"The nine food places have five on one side and four on the other," he explained.

Only one of the nine places looked like it wasn't going to be lots of sugar. They walked up to Harry's Hamburgers and looked at the menu.

The first item on the menu:

Harry's Huge One-pound Burger. Sixteen ounces of prime ground beef. Enough to fill the biggest tummy.

Betty looked at Fred. He shook his head and thought: *That's enough food to last me for a whole month.*

The second item on the menu:

Harry's Half-pound Burger. Eight ounces of great meat with catsup, lettuce, tomatoes, and a pickle.

Betty looked at Fred. He shook his head and thought: *Only some big giant would eat that much.*

The third item on the menu:

Harry's Four-ounce Burger.

Fred shook his head. *That's what a normal full-sized adult might eat.*

The fourth item: Harry's Two-ounce Burger.
Fred told Betty that he wasn't that hungry.

The fifth item: Harry's One-ounce Baby Burger.
Fred: "No thank you."

The sixth item: Harry's Half-ounce Burger Bite.
Fred: "Too much food."

The seventh item: Harry's Burger Crumb. One tenth of an ounce of beef. You will hardly notice that you have eaten it.
Before Fred could refuse, Betty ordered: "I'd like a Four-ounce Burger for myself and a Burger Crumb for Fred."

"And what would you like to drink?" the man behind the counter asked.
Before Fred could say the bad word, Betty put her hand over his mouth and said, "We would like two glasses of milk."

"May I please have a straw?" Fred asked the man behind the counter.

"Sorry, we're out of straws," he replied.

As they sat at a table, Betty was eating her Four-ounce Burger and drinking her milk. Fred was letting his Burger Crumb cool off.

Fred was in no hurry to eat.

He took out a pencil. Betty suggested that he might drink some milk rather than draw.

He borrowed some scissors from Betty and began to cut a long strip of paper.

He wound it around the pencil.

And glued it. And waited for it to dry. Betty was almost done with her hamburger and milk. Fred was still playing at the table instead of eating.

When it was dry, he pulled the pencil out and said, "Look! I have a straw."

He put the straw into his milk and tried to drink. As the milk went up the straw, it wet the paper. The straw fell apart.

By this time, his Burger Crumb was cold and his glass of milk had paper and glue floating in it.

Time Out!

The year was 1888. Marvin Stone did what Fred had done. He wound a strip of paper around a pencil. He glued it.

Except Marvin used stiffer paper that had wax on it.

Marvin Stone invented the world's first paper straw.

Your Turn to Play

1. It took Fred 5 minutes to cut the paper and wind it around the pencil. It took 4 minutes to glue it and let the glue dry. How long did it take Fred to make his straw? $5 + 4 = ?$

2.  Betty had finished her meal. Fred had a cold Burger Crumb and a glass of milk with a mess in it. What time was it?

3. To do the previous problem, you had to count to 40 by fives. If a package of gum has 5 sticks, how many sticks are in 8 packages?

·······ANSWERS·······

1. 5 minutes plus 4 minutes equals 9 minutes.

2.  It is 40 minutes after 5 o'clock. 5:40 or 5:40 p.m.

3.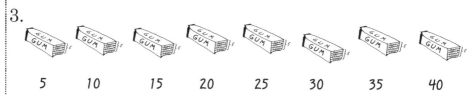

    Counting by fives is a lot quicker than counting each stick of gum:

$$^{1}2_{3}4_{5} \qquad ^{6}78_{9}10 \qquad ^{11}12_{13}14_{15} \qquad ^{16}17_{18}19_{20} \qquad ^{21}22_{23}24_{25} \qquad ^{26}27_{28}29_{30} \qquad ^{31}32_{33}34_{35} \qquad ^{36}37_{38}39_{40}$$

A big secret

    Right now you are learning the addition tables. In the previous book you learned all the ways to add to seven: $7 + 0 = 7$; $6 + 1 = 7$; $5 + 2 = 7$; $4 + 3 = 7$.

    In a year or so after you have learned everything up to $9 + 9$, you will learn the multiplication tables. This will be almost like magic. Instead of adding up eight fives $(5 + 5 + 5 + 5 + 5 + 5 + 5 + 5)$, you will learn that eight times five equals 40. $8 \times 5 = 40$.

Chapter Six
The Hunter

Fred put the Burger Crumb in his pocket. He would eat it later if he got hungry.

Over the last four years, Betty had seen Fred do this many times. Fred would stick food in his pocket and say, "For later."

Betty and Fred headed outside into the cool, dark Kansas evening.

When they got away from the lights of the buildings, they could see the stars.

Fred pointed. "Look. There's Orion's* belt! That is one of the easiest things to spot in the winter sky. Three stars all in a row."

—A Small Story—

Years ago . . . before computers, before television, before movies, before radio, there were people. In fact, most people who have ever lived have never heard of these things.

Instead of spending hours watching television, they went outside to see what was playing in the night sky.

———————————————

* Or-EYE-in's

Instead of being entertained, they entertained themselves. They looked up at the sky and saw those three stars. Someone thought those three stars looked like a belt.

During the daytime, you might see clouds that looked like camels or faces, but they would be soon gone.

But every night there was that belt.

Then someone noticed that if that was a belt, then let's put a sword on that belt. It's amazing what you start to see when you look at something for many hours.

Then someone saw the body.

 Most people nowadays can see the belt and maybe the sword. If you stare at it for five minutes, you could find the four stars that make up the body, but it doesn't look much like a body.

But look at those stars for hours each night, and you add a head and arms. It becomes Orion, the Hunter—one of the most famous constellations in the sky.

Now the fun part begins.
Look at Orion's shoulder. ———
That is a star worth knowing about.

That star is Betelgeuse.*

Betelgeuse is a red supergiant star.
Our sun   is a star. It
looks different   because we are
so close to it.** Our sun is big and
yellow. The stars look like little points
of light because they are so far away.

But Betelgeuse is much bigger than our sun. It is
one of the largest stars known. How big? If our sun were
the size of an orange, then Betelgeuse would be the size of
a football stadium.

It's big.

—end of Small Story—

"It would be fun to invent my own
constellation," Betty said. "I once read a list of
all the official constellations. There are less than
a hundred of them. I remember the list began:
Andromeda, Antlia, Apus, and Aquarius."

She looked up at the sky and tried to
imagine a picture.

----

* Pronounced *beetle juice*.

** We are only 93,000,000 miles away from it. In words: ninety-three
million miles.

One group of stars looked like a television set. Another looked like a bottle of nail polish.

Finally, she picked three stars out of the Orion constellation.

"What are you going to call your new constellation?" Fred asked.

"I'll call it Betty's Triangle. If you connect the three dots, it does make a triangle."

Betty giggled. "And I'll make a constellation for my boyfriend Alexander and one for you."

Alexander is six feet tall, and Fred is only three feet tall, so Alexander's constellation was bigger than Fred's.

Fred liked the idea of having his own constellation.

Fred's Triangle

Alexander's Triangle

Your Turn to Play

1. Fred thought about making a constellation for each of the students in the classes he taught. He could make one for Darlene, one for Joe, etc.

   At first, he thought he could make a constellation by picking out any three stars in the sky and making a triangle.

   Then he realized that was wrong. You can't just pick out any three stars and make a triangle. When wouldn't that work?

2. Alexander is 6 feet tall. Fred is 3 feet tall. If you put Fred on top of Alexander, they would be 9 feet tall. We could write this: $6 + 3 = 9$.

   If Fred were really, really, really strong, you could put Alexander on top of Fred. $3 + 6 = ?$

3. What time is it?

4. $5 + 2 = ?$

5. $5 + 4 = ?$

. . . . ANSWERS . . . .

1. You can't make a triangle with three stars if the stars are all in a row (like Orion's belt).

The fancy name in math for three points that are all in a row is **collinear**. (co-LYNN-knee-er)

These three points are collinear.

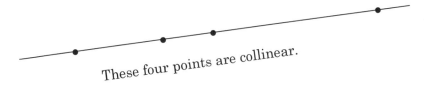

These four points are collinear.

2. 3 + 6 = 9

3.

It is 45 minutes past 5 or 5:45.

(In 15 minutes it will be six o'clock.)

4. 5 + 2 = 7

5. 5 + 4 = 9

Chapter Seven
For Later

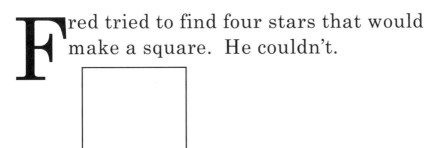

red tried to find four stars that would make a square. He couldn't.

Sometimes he could find three stars that might work, but there was no fourth star.

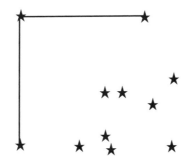

Triangles are easy. Squares are hard. Almost any three stars could make a triangle. Almost no four stars would make a square.

At this point Betty still hadn't asked about the calculus problem $\int \frac{1}{x^3+1}\, dx$.

Like the Burger Crumb in Fred's pocket, it would be "for later."

Unlike the Burger Crumb in Fred's pocket, Betty would ask Fred about $\int \frac{1}{x^3 + 1}\, dx$ in class tomorrow. She really meant "for later."

When Fred put a piece of food in his pocket, his "for later" became "for . . . never."

When his pockets became full of food, he would empty his pockets into a drawer in his desk. Then the ants would find it.

Instead of "for later," an ant would say

Ants never say, "For later." They do not put off things for tomorrow that they could do today.

It was a Monday evening on the KITTENS University campus in Kansas. In five minutes it would be 6 p.m.

It was 5:55 p.m.

They stopped at the campus bulletin board and read the sign:

Coming Events

at KITTENS

Sunday 6 p.m.

Hot Dog
Eating Contest

Monday 6 p.m. Prof.
Eldwood book signing
at the library. It's his
newest book.

Since it was Monday, they had missed the hot dog eating contest, which was on Sunday. But they were not too late to go to the book signing.

In five minutes they walked to the KITTENS library. It was 6 p.m.

"There's Alexander!" Betty exclaimed.

They got together, and Betty told Alexander about the caterpillars in Fred's office, about the eggs on Kingie's hat, and about the song that Fred had sung to Kingie to help him get to sleep.

She didn't mention the paper straw that Fred had made.

"Oh," she said. "I've got to show you something outside."

She turned to Fred and said, "We'll be back in a second."

That was fine with Fred. He had already seen Orion, the Hunter. He knew that she was going to show him Alexander's Triangle, which went from the left star in Orion's belt to the two legs of Orion.

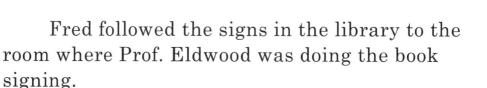

Fred followed the signs in the library to the room where Prof. Eldwood was doing the book signing.

Book signings are not just watching an author autograph his books. That would be boring. Mainly, it is a chance to talk with an author about his work. You can also buy his book and have him sign it.

Fred walked into the room where the book signing was happening.*

There was a big sign on the wall: "Prof. Eldwood's newest book: *The Names for Toenail in 300 Languages.*"

Fred wondered how many people would like to buy that book. It didn't seem like a very popular title.

Fred was the only person in the room.

Your Turn to Play

1. This is five minutes to six o'clock. Draw a clock that would show five minutes to three o'clock.

2. When Betty met Alexander, she told him about the caterpillars in Fred's office, about the eggs on Kingie's hat, and about the song that Fred had sung to Kingie. She didn't mention the paper straw that Fred had made. Make a guess why she didn't mention the straw.

---

* My English teacher in the 7th grade once took a point off when I wrote, "He walked *in* the room." It is supposed to be *into* the room.

· · · · · · · ANSWERS · · · · · · ·

1. This is five minutes to three o'clock. It is 2:55.

2. There are several possible reasons. Your answer may be different than mine.

✓ She may have just forgotten about that incident.

✓ She may not have wanted to embarrass Fred by talking about something he did that failed.

✓ She may have been eager to go and show Alexander the Alexander Triangle constellation. She *deliberately* cut short the full story of everything that had recently happened.

✓ Recall that she said, "Oh, I've got to show you something outside." That seems to indicate that the thought of Alexander's Triangle had suddenly occurred to her, and she *inadvertently* forgot about telling the rest of what had happened with Fred and her.

Deliberate vs. Inadvertent

Deliberate and inadvertent are opposites. When you do something deliberately, you are choosing to do something—your brain is working. You choose to write an email to a friend.

When you inadvertently do something, you weren't paying attention—your brain was somewhere else.

If you deliberately broke a vase, that is much different than if you inadvertently broke it.

Chapter Eight
First, Second . . .

In front of the big sign on the wall was a table. On it was a small stack of books. There was no one else in the room. Fred walked over and looked at one of the books.

The Names
for
Toenail
in
300 Languages

Prof. Eldwood

Fred opened the book. On each of the 300 pages was a name for toenail in a different language.

On the German page: der Zehennagel.

Fred thought to himself: *You never know when such a book might come in handy. Suppose I were traveling in Norway and I needed to tell someone about my toenail. I would really need this book.*

At the age of five, Fred thought there were only two kinds of books:

First kind: the books I own,

Second kind: the books I want to own.

There is a third kind of book: those that would be a waste of money to buy. Fred had some of those books in his office:

Using a Yak to Move Your Yurt,*

Famous Tennis Trophies,

Muscle Shoals: Which Used to Be a Rapids But Is Now a Lake Because of the Wilson Dam.

First, second, third, fourth . . . is a different way of counting. They are called **ordinal numbers** because they talk about the *order* that things come in.

Fred wondered why Prof. Eldwood's book wasn't selling. He thought that the room should be crowded with people wanting to buy lots of copies of his book.

They could buy a copy for themselves and several other copies to give as birthday presents.

---

* A yurt is a round dwelling—poles covered with felt or skins—used in parts of central Asia.

Fred thought: *Maybe if Prof. Eldwood arranged his books differently. Then they might sell better.*

There was a stack of nine books on the table. To Fred, that didn't seem very attractive. He moved four of the books to the left side of the table and left five of them on the right side.

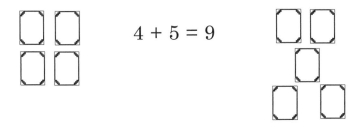

$$4 + 5 = 9$$

Then Fred thought: *What if a couple came in and they each wanted to buy a book? There should be two books waiting just for them.*

He put two books on the left side and seven on the right.

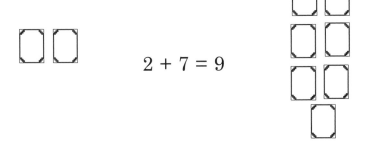

$$2 + 7 = 9$$

"Hey, sonny.* I see you like my books." It was Prof. Eldwood. He was really old. It was rumored that some of his books were written in the 1840s. That was hard to believe.

"I see you have put seven of the books in a pile on the right side of my desk," he continued. "I'm guessing those are the ones you want to buy for yourself and your friends."

That made sense to Fred. He counted: one for myself, one for Kingie, and then copies to Betty, Alexander, Joe, and Darlene, and one extra copy.

"That comes to 35 cents," Prof. Eldwood said. (That is sometimes written as 35¢.)

Fred had a bunch of nickels in his pocket. (They are worth 5¢ each.)

He counted out 35¢:

5   10   15   20   25   30   35

---

* *Sonny* is what some old men call five-year-old boys.

Please remember to write out your answers before looking on the next page.

Your Turn to Play

1. Yes. Fred bought 7 copies of *The Names for* Toenail *in 300 Languages.* Prof. Eldwood started out with 9 copies. After Fred bought 7 of them, how many did Prof. Eldwood have left?

2. Write the ordinal numbers up to tenth. Here is a start: first, second, third, fourth.

3. Joe and Darlene are two other students that Fred has. (You will hear a lot about them in later *Life of Fred* adventures.) Joe once told Darlene that *Monday* is the only day of the week with six letters in it. Was he right?

4. How many nickels does it take to make 35¢? (Count the coins on the previous page.)

. . . . **ANSWERS** . . . .

1. If Fred bought the 7 books on the right side, that left 2 books on the left side.

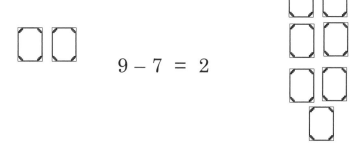

$$9 - 7 = 2$$

2. First, second, third, fourth, fifth, sixth, seventh, eighth, ninth, tenth.

The one that some people misspell is *ninth*. There is no "e" in ninth.

3. Joe was not right.

Sunday	6 letters
Monday	6 letters
Tuesday	
Wednesday	
Thursday	
Friday	6 letters
Saturday	

This is the set of all the days of the week that have six letters in them: {Sunday, Monday, Friday}.

4. Seven nickels. Seven 5s make 35.

Chapter Nine
Campus Mail

Fred took his seven copies down the library hallway and deposited them in the campus mailbox. KITTENS campus mail is a little different than ordinary mail:

First, mailboxes are almost everywhere. You are never more than 50 yards from a box.

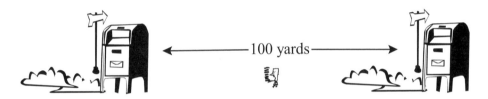

Second, KITTENS campus mail is free.
Students liked attending KITTENS University.
They show their gratitude by volunteering.
Some of them mow the lawns. Some help in the offices. And some deliver the campus mail.

Third, KITTENS campus mail is fast. Whenever any mail is deposited in a box, a special light on the top of the box turns on.

Student letter carriers rush over to the box and get the mail and run to deliver it.

Fred then headed back to the book-signing room to meet Betty and Alexander. They were just coming out of that room. They each had a copy of Prof. Eldwood's book in their hands.

"Hi, Fred!" Betty said. "We just bought the last two books that Prof. Eldwood had. He said that sales of his book have been really great, and that someone had just come in and purchased seven copies."

Fred realized that he wouldn't be giving any of his copies to Betty and Alexander. He would have one for his own library, one for Kingie, and two to give to his students Darlene and Joe.

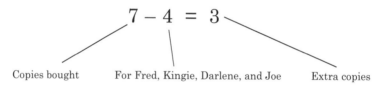

$$7 - 4 = 3$$

Copies bought   For Fred, Kingie, Darlene, and Joe   Extra copies

He had three copies more than he needed.

Fred, Betty, and Alexander walked down the library hallway. They stopped at the mailbox. The light on the top of the mailbox was not on since the student letter carriers had already come and picked up the seven copies that Fred had mailed.

Betty said that she was giving her copy to Darlene. Alexander addressed his copy to Joe. They dropped them into the mailbox.

Fred had a lot of copies of *The Names for Toenail in 300 Languages* and no one except Kingie to give them to.

They headed out of the library, and Alexander said, "Hey. Have you guys had dinner yet? It's after six o'clock, and I haven't eaten since lunch.

"Fred and I have been to the food court," Betty said. "But we would be happy to join you."

Alexander didn't get to be six feet tall by skipping meals

6:15

and drinking a lot of sugary Sluice. They headed back to Harry's Hamburgers. Alexander ordered Harry's Half-pound Burger and a large glass of milk.

They sat down at a table. Fred wondered if he was hungry yet. He hadn't eaten all day. He took his Harry's Burger Crumb out of his pocket and put it on the table. He looked at it for a moment and then put it back in his pocket "for later."

As Alexander munched into his half-pound hamburger, Betty turned to Fred and said, "Alexander really liked the constellation I named after him."

After Alexander swallowed, he said, "One of the really neat things is that Alexander's Triangle includes Orion's sword that hangs down from his belt—three stars inside my constellation."

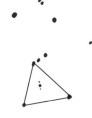

"Two," said Fred.

Betty and Alexander looked at Fred. They didn't understand. Finally, Betty asked, "Two what?"

"Two stars in Orion's sword," Fred answered.

They couldn't believe that this five-year-old math professor couldn't count up to three. Alexander finished his hamburger and milk in a hurry, and the three of them headed outside to count the stars in Orion's sword.

Outside, Fred counted, "One, Two stars."

"Hey! You skipped the middle one," Alexander said.

Fred smiled.

Fred had an advantage over those twenty-year-olds. His eyes were young. He told them to look at those three "stars" in the sword.

Eye Test

Look at the middle "star" in the sword. Does it look fuzzy? If so, you have great eyes. It isn't a star!

Your Turn to Play

1. $7 - 4 = 3$ is true because $4 + 3 = 7$.

    Why is $9 - 4 = 5$ true?

2. What day of the week has the most letters?

3. How many nickels would it take to equal 25¢?

4. What is the ordinal number that follows fifth?

5. Translate from German into English: der Zehennagel.

6. What time is it?

. . . . ANSWERS . . . .

1. $9 - 4 = 5$ is true because $4 + 5 = 9$.

2. Sunday   6 letters

   Monday   6 letters

   Tuesday   7 letters

   Wednesday   9 letters   The winner!

   Thursday   8 letters

   Friday   6 letters

   Saturday   8 letters

3.

   5   10   15   20   25

   Five nickels.

4. After *fifth* comes *sixth*.

5. der Zehennagel = (the) toenail

6. 6:30

   Some people say this is "half past six."

Chapter Ten
Orion Nebula

That bit of fuzziness that Alexander thought was a star was the **Great Orion Nebula.**[*] It is a cloud of glowing dust and gas. A big cloud.

It is 24 light years across.

Time Out!

A **light year** is the distance that light can travel in a year. It is a distance, not a time.

Since light can go 186,000 miles in one second, a light year is a long distance.

Since there are 60 seconds in a minute, light can go sixty times as far in a minute. Later, when you learn multiplication, you will be able to multiply 186,000 times 60.

---

[*] That's actually the old-fashioned name for it. Nowadays they just call it the Orion Nebula. Astronomers call it Messier 42 or sometimes just M42.

Since there are 60 minutes in an hour, and 24 hours in a day, and 365.25 days in a year (That period in 365.25 is called a decimal point. You'll also learn about that later)—it all multiplies to about 6 trillion miles in a light year.

6,000,000,000,000 miles
equals one light year.

So that big cloud of glowing dust and gas—the Orion Nebula—is 24 light years across. If you use binoculars to look at the middle "star" in Orion's sword, it's much easier to see that it is fuzzy and not like the other two stars in the sword.

The Orion Nebula is one of the most photographed things in the sky.

It takes a little over one second for light to travel from the moon to the earth. When you look at the moon, you are seeing it as it was one second ago.

It takes a little over eight minutes for the light from the sun to reach us. If the sun suddenly turned purple, we would know about it eight minutes after it happened.

The bunch of stars known as the
Andromeda Galaxy is about 2,500,000 light years
away from us. Light from stars in the
Andromeda Galaxy takes about 2,500,000 years
to reach us.

As they walked, they decided to play a
game. Alexander suggested they count the
stars.*

Alexander started: 1, 2, 3, 4, 5, 6. . . .
Betty counted by 2s: 2, 4, 6, 8, 10. . . .
Fred counted by 5s: 5, 10, 15, 20, 25. . . .

After they got tired of counting the stars,
Fred said that he could count in a different way:

First, he said 1.
Then 1,000.   one thousand
Then 1,000,000   one million
Then 1,000,000,000   one billion
Then 1,000,000,000,000   one trillion

Then Betty suggested they play the
Alphabet game. One person suggested a

---

* On a clear, dark night, you might be able to see about 4,000 (four thousand) stars. If
you use binoculars, you can see a lot more. If you use a telescope, you can see zillions
of stars.

category, and then they took turns saying the alphabet in that category.

Alexander suggested the category of Food.

Fred said, "Apricot."

Betty said, "Banana."

Alexander said, "Cake."

Fred: "Doughnut."

Betty: "Egg."

Alexander: "Fudge."

They got stuck when they got to X.*

Then Fred suggested "States in the United States" as the category for the Alphabet game.

Fred: "Alabama."

Betty was stuck. She couldn't think of a state starting with B.

She suggested they restart the game using "Countries" instead of "States in the United States."

Fred: "Albania."

Betty: "Bolivia."

Alexander: "Canada."

Fred: "Denmark."

---

* For Q, they said, "Quince," which is a yellowish fruit used in making jelly.

Betty: "Estonia."

Alexander: "France."

Fred: "Germany."

Betty: "Hungary."

Alexander giggled and said, "No I'm not. I had a big hamburger." He was playing. He knew that Betty had said the country of Hungary and not, "Hungry."

Your Turn to Play

1. Some categories for the Alphabet game are easier to play than others.

   If you and your friends are artists, then Colors might be a good category: Azure, Blue, Carmine. . . .

   You might use First Names of People: Adam, Bill, Carrie, Dennis, Elizabeth, Fred, George, Harry. . . .

   You might use animals.

   You might use things found in the house.

   Or things you can pick up with tongs.

   Name a category that would be really hard to use.

2. 4 + 5 = ?

3. 3 apples plus 6 apples equals how many apples?

4. How many nickels equal 45¢?

5. Which day of the week comes right before Wednesday?

·······ANSWERS·······

1. Your answer might be different than mine.
A category that would be really hard to use would be:

✓ The Days of the Week. (There are none that begin with A.)

✓ Words in German. (Unless, of course, you know German.)

✓ The Names of Cars Made in South America.

✓ Names of Norwegian Women. (Unless, of course, you know a lot of people from Norway.)

2. $4 + 5 = 9$

3. Three apples plus six apples equals nine apples because $3 + 6 = 9$.

4. You need 9 nickels to make 45¢.

 5   10   15   20   25   30   35   40   45

5. Sunday
   Monday
   Tuesday ◀——— comes right before Wednesday
   Wednesday
   Thursday
   Friday
   Saturday

Chapter Eleven
The Bell Tower

Fred liked walking with his two friends in the evening. The KITTENS University campus was a perfect place to walk. There were lots of paths. They went through groves of trees, to the buildings, to the tennis courts, the chapel, the student center, the rose gardens, and the bell tower.

Every hour the bell tower would chime. The giant bell would tell the hour with a deep, mellow bong.

If it were  you would hear, "Bong. Bong."

As they walked, they heard the bell tower starting to chime. Betty asked, "Is it seven o'clock already? It seems like it was just 6:30 a second ago."

They listened.

Bong. Bong. Bong. Bong. Bong. Bong. Bong.

"It must be seven o'clock," Alexander announced.

But the bell tower continued: Bong. Bong. Bong. Bong. Bong. Bong. Bong. Bong. Bong. Bong. Bong. Bong. Bong. Bong. Bong. Bong.

They looked at each other with fear and bewilderment.*

Fred had seen that same look once before when he accidentally handed his arithmetic class a calculus test. They were expecting $4 + 3 = ?$ and $9 - 2 = ?$ Instead they received:

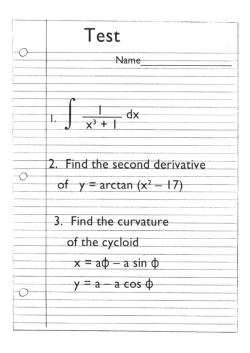

Typical arithmetic
student's reaction to
receiving this calculus test

The bell got quieter: Bong. Bing. Bong-bingy-bong. Bing. Boop. Bing. Bingy-bong. Bing. Boop.

---

* Bewildered = confused + puzzled + mystified

They had been in one of the woods on campus when they first heard the bell tower. Alexander ran down the path to get a clear view of the bell tower. Betty was right behind him.

Alexander was six feet tall and had long legs. He could run quickly.

Fred's legs were part of his three-foot body. But he moved his legs twice as fast as Alexander.

Each of them was thinking something different.

Alexander was thinking that there may be an electrical problem in the tower.

Betty was thinking that the tower might be on fire.

Fred was thinking that a whole bunch of butterflies had flown inside the tower and had laid their eggs on the bell.

The three of them arrived at a clearing at almost the same time.

None of their guesses had been right. The truth was stranger than any of them thought.

The bell tower was starting to tip over.

Alexander thought about calling 9-1-1 on his cell phone, but the batteries were dead.

Fred thought about pushing on the building to straighten it, but nobody is *that strong*.

Betty remembered that Ned's office was nearby. They all ran over to his place. He had a big flashing, neon sign in front of his office.

NEDRICK A. WISTROM

BUILDING AND GROUNDS
NIGHT DIVISION

Nedrick's job was to handle anything that happened at night. He would stay awake all night and sleep during the daytime. Some people called him Ned, the Night Guy.

Betty knocked on his door.

Ned answered the door. He said, "Hi Betty. I was just having breakfast." He knew Betty's name. On a small college campus, everyone knows almost everyone else.

Betty began, "I think we may have a problem with one of the buildings."

Fred had a lot to learn about being an adult. He was in an absolute panic. He was shaking.

He would have told Ned, "You won't believe it! There is something really, horribly, terribly bad happening outside! You gotta see it! I've never seen anything like it! Come quick and look for yourself!"

Betty was cool. With her dozen words, she told Ned a lot more than Fred would have with his 29 words.

Your Turn to Play

1. Betty's dozen words: "I think we may have a problem with one of the buildings."

How many is a dozen?

2. If Fred wasn't in a panic, he might have sputtered out something like, "The Bell Tower is not perpendicular to the ground." (purr-pen-DICK-you-lure)

Ned would have responded, "That's mighty peculiar. You say it's not perpendicular. What's perpendicular?"

Ned had never learned any geometry. He had been hired because he liked to stay up during the night.

"Things are perpendicular if they form right angles," Fred explained.

Ned scratched his head and said, "Is that right? What's a right angle?"

"It's like the corner of a square."

 Can you find perpendicular lines on Fred's head?

·······ANSWERS·······

1.   1   2   3   4
"I think we may

   5   6   7   8
have a problem with

   9   10   11   12
one of the buildings."

A dozen equals 12.

Eggs are often sold as a dozen.

There are a dozen hours on a clock.

There are a dozen months in a year.

2.   Here is one pair
of perpendicular lines.

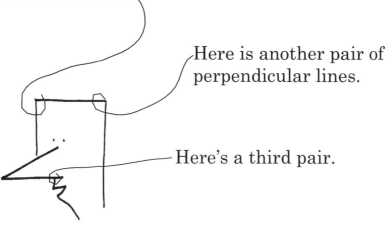

Here is another pair of
perpendicular lines.

Here's a third pair.

Chapter Twelve
Talking with Ned

Ned took the napkin he had tucked in his shirt and wiped some of the breakfast cereal off of his mouth. Instead of using milk on his cereal, he used Sluice. The sugar in the Sluice made the cereal stick to his face.

"Is that so?" Ned said in response to Betty's dozen words.[*]

Ned had never had much education. He never read anything except the TV listings. The only reason he got his job was that no one else wanted to stay awake all night. From 6 p.m. to 6 a.m. he ate and watched television.[**]

Ned liked saying things like: "Is that so?"

"Interesting."

"Really."

"Mighty peculiar."

"Is that right?"

because he didn't have much to contribute to any

---

[*] (1) I (2) think (3) we (4) may (5) have (6) a (7) problem (8) with (9) one (10) of (11) our (12) buildings.

[**] "a.m." means before noon. "p.m." means after noon—between noon and midnight. In Latin, p.m. stands for *post meridiem.*

P.M. means something entirely different than p.m. P.M. means Paymaster or Postmaster or Prime Minister.

conversation, and those words would encourage the other person to talk.

"It's the bell tower," Betty continued.

"Oh?" Ned said, trying to look concerned.

This conversation was going too slowly for Fred. He was starting to wiggle. He would stand on one foot and then the other.

He pointed upward.

Then he moved his arm downward, trying to convey the idea of a building falling over.

Alexander took a hold of one of Fred's hands to quiet him down. Everyone knew that Betty could do the best job of conveying to eleven-hours-of-television-a-day Ned the idea that the bell tower was falling over.

Betty eschewed the jargon of "orthogonality" and "impending structural devolution."

Betty stayed away from the language of "things being at right angles" and "upcoming passing of a building from one stage to another."

Rather than try to explain to Ned what was happening and hearing him say, "interesting," and "really," she asked him to come outside and look at the bell tower.

"Do I have time to finish my cereal first?" Ned asked.

This was too much for Fred. A building was falling down and Ned asked if he could finish his cereal first.

Fred experienced syncope.* Alexander picked Fred up and held him in his arms.

Betty thought about informing Ned of the inadvisability of delaying Ned's inspection and responded, "No. I think you should see the bell tower right now."

"Really?" Ned asked.

"Really!" Betty answered.

"Oh," Ned said.

"You see, Ned," Betty explained. "I think it's tipping over."

"Interesting," Ned said.

---

* SING-ka-pee   Syncope = fainting   When medical doctors are writing research papers for journals, they use a lot of jargon (the special language of their occupation). They might write "a brief loss of consciousness caused by insufficient flow of blood to the brain" or they might write "syncope," but all their buddies would laugh at them if they wrote "fainting."

Besides, *syncope* has only seven letters. *Fainting* has eight. So it's shorter to write *syncope.*

Ned turned off the television in his dining room, the one in the living room, and the one in the bathroom. Then Ned, Betty, Alexander, and Fred headed outside to see the bell tower.

By this time Fred had regained consciousness. He liked being carried by Alexander so he kept his eyes shut for a while. Since he only weighed 37 pounds, he was lighter than some groceries that Alexander would sometimes carry.*

When they got to the bell tower, Ned said, "Mighty peculiar." He did not mention the lack of orthogonality with respect to the ground.

It was this ————————————— not this.

orthogonal lines

---

* During the summer, Alexander would often buy five-pound watermelons at the store. If he got 8 of them, they would weigh 40 pounds since eight times five is forty.
$$8 \times 5 = 40.$$

Or, since you have not had multiplication yet, $5 + 5 + 5 + 5 + 5 + 5 + 5 + 5 = 40$. People who have learned their multiplication tables can look at this clock and say 12:40 instead of counting by fives: 5, 10, 15, 20, 25, 30, 35, 40. Eight 5s are 40.

Ned stared at the bell tower for several minutes. Betty, Alexander, and Fred imagined that Ned was in deep thought.

At first, Ned thought: *That thing ain't square.*

Then he thought about his cereal.

Then about the television program he was missing.

Then he realized he was standing in front of a building that was tipping over and three people were looking at him for guidance.

He said, "Interesting."

Your Turn to Play

1. The ability to concentrate and not have your mind wander around is one thing a good education gives you. It takes some concentration to answer the question: If yesterday was Thursday, what day will tomorrow be?

Rather than say, "Interesting," answer the question.

2. If you had a dozen eggs in a carton and took two of them out of the carton, how many would be left in the carton?

3. How many perpendicular lines are in this face? ☺

4. Write down a sentence that has exactly a dozen words in it.

5. $4 + 5 = ?$

.......ANSWERS.......

1. Sunday
   Monday
   Tuesday
   Wednesday
   Thursday
   Friday   If yesterday was Thursday
   Saturday   tomorrow will be Saturday

2. You start with 12 eggs
and you take out 2 of them.
Count backwards: 12, 11, 10.

$$12 - 2 = 10$$

3. There aren't any straight lines in ☺
so there can't be any perpendicular lines.
There are zero pairs of perpendicular lines in ☺.

4. Your answer may differ from mine. Here are several
sentences I thought of with a dozen words in them:

#1: Write down a sentence that has exactly a dozen
words in it.

#2: He slept and slept and slept and slept and slept and
slept.

#3: You can never have your dreams come true unless
you wake up.

5. $4 + 5 = 9$

Chapter Thirteen
Who to Call?

Ned really didn't know what to do. If there was a plumbing leak, he would call the plumber. If there was a fire or a medical emergency, he would dial 9-1-1.

He walked back to his office and looked in the campus phone directory.

ART DEPARTMENT . . . Ned thought: *They would just come and draw pictures of it.*

MUSIC DEPARTMENT . . . Ned thought: *They would compose a symphony.*

The Crash of the Bell Tower

NEWS DEPARTMENT—CAMPUS NEWSPAPER . . . Ned thought: *That's it! This is certainly news.*

Ned called The KITTEN Caboodle newspaper.

Faster than Ned could say "That's interesting," the newspaper sent out a reporter and a photographer.

THE KITTEN Caboodle

The Official Campus Newspaper of KITTENS University   Monday 6:55 p.m.   10¢

late-breaking news

Bell Tower Is Falling

KANSAS: Minutes ago, Nedrick A. Wistrom, head of Building and Grounds—Night Division, reported that the campus bell tower was tipping over.

Our Caboodle reporter interviewed people from the mob that had gathered in the early evening hours to witness the disaster.

Wistrom, also known around our campus as Ned, the Night Guy, announced, "It's mighty peculiar."

Prof. Fred Glass said, "Buildings should be orthogonal with respect to the earth."

Eye Witness
Fred Goose

advertisement

Waddle's Doughnuts

Buy a dozen
and get
one free.

13 for the price of 12!

When Wistrom was asked who had been contacted regarding this calamity, he mentioned something about the television program he was missing.

On the KITTENS campus, the newspaper was published as fast as greased lightning.

Just after the reporter and photographer left, Betty got a copy of the newspaper. She shook her head. "What poor reporting," she exclaimed. "They couldn't get Fred's last name right. Everyone on campus knows that he is Fred Gauss[*]—not Glass or Goose. And they called us a 'mob.' That's a disorderly crowd of people. We were just standing there watching the building lean over."

Time Out!

Almost everybody knows about quotation marks (" "). You put them around what someone actually said.

For example, Chris said, "Hi."

What happens when you have a quotation inside of a quotation? In the paragraph above this box, we are quoting Betty, and Betty is quoting the newspaper. The inside quotation gets single quotation marks (' ').

For example, Pat told Jackie, "Chris said 'Hi' to me."

---

[*] *Gauss* rhymes with *house.*

As Alexander read his copy of the newspaper, he commented, "They didn't even get a picture of the building. And the paper called it a 'disaster.' That's crazy. The building is just leaning over. It would be a disaster if it fell."

> single quotation mark

> double quotation mark

The bell tower sounded quietly: Bong-bingy-bong. Bingy-bong. Boop.

Alexander turned to Ned and asked him, "Whom have you called?"

Ned answered, "About what?"

"About the bell tower!" Alexander almost shouted.

"Well . . . Just the newspaper," Ned said.

Alexander couldn't believe it. He said, "Don't you think someone should be notified?"

"Really?" Ned said. "I'll leave a note for Ralph." Ned put a sticky note that read "**bell tower**" on Ralph's door and then headed back to his office to turn on his three TVs and finish his cereal. Ralph was Ned's brother. He had an office right next to Ned's. His office also had a big flashing sign in front of it.

RALPH L. WISTROM

BUILDING AND GROUNDS

DAY DIVISION

From 6 a.m. to 6 p.m. Ralph would sit in his office and watch television and eat. Neither Ralph nor Ned ever *did* anything of importance.

Your Turn to Play

1. Ralph works the dozen hours between 6 a.m. and 6 p.m. One day he worked from 6 a.m. to 7 p.m., which is one more hour than a dozen. How many hours did he work that day?

2. If tomorrow is Wednesday, what day was yesterday?

3. If Fred had any hair and he got a really short haircut (known as a crewcut or a buzz cut), the hairs on the top of his head would be orthogonal to the top of his head. Draw a picture of how Fred would look.

4. $3 + 6 = ?$

5. $5 + 4 = ?$

. . . . ANSWERS . . . .

1. A dozen plus one more is 13.

$$12 + 1 = 13$$

Thirteen is sometimes called a baker's dozen. One story of why 13 is called a baker's dozen goes back about 800 years ago to King Henry III in England. Henry III made a law that any baker who cheated his customers by giving them 11 items and calling it a dozen could have really bad things done to him. Really bad things—that should only be mentioned to readers in high school and beyond.

The bakers were so frightened of the really bad things that could happen to them that they often gave their customers 13 for the price of 12. It became known as a baker's dozen.

2. Sunday

   Monday

   Tuesday   If tomorrow is Wednesday, then

   Wednesday   yesterday would be Monday.

   Thursday

   Friday

   Saturday

3. Fred looks silly with hair.

4. $3 + 6 = 9$

5. $5 + 4 = 9$

Chapter Fourteen
Quotes within Quotes

Fred liked the idea of having quotations within quotations. That seemed like so much fun when Alexander said, "The newspaper called it a 'disaster.' "

He asked Betty what she would do if she had a quote within a quote within a quote. He knew that the first quote would have double quotation marks (" ") and the second inside quote would have single quotation marks (' '). He wondered what the third quote inside the second quote inside the first quote would look like.

She told him that the rule in English is that you alternate. You go back-and-forth between double and single quotes.

Fred thought for a moment and giggled. Then he said to Betty, "My Sunday School teacher told me yesterday in the Book of Acts, 'Peter once told a crowd of people, "The Prophet Joel once said, 'In the last days, God says, "I will pour out my Spirit on all people." ' " ' "

Time Out!

This sentence that Fred just spoke has got to be the world's record for putting quotes inside of quotes. Fred had five quotations tucked inside each other.

In a whole lifetime of reading, you will probably never see that record beaten.

You could email a friend of yours and write, "Today I saw the world's record number of quotes within quotes in my *Life of Fred: Butterflies* book which said, 'Then he said to Betty, "My Sunday School teacher told me yesterday in the Book of Acts, 'Peter once told a crowd of people, "The Prophet Joel once said, 'In the last days, God says, "I will pour out my Spirit on all people." ' " ' " ' "

Seven quotes within quotes.

It was 8 p.m. Ned's sticky note that read **"belltower"** was on Ralph's door. Ned was watching television. Ralph was sleeping.

And the bell tower fell down.

There used to be four Wistrom brothers who worked at KITTENS University: Samuel, Lawrence, Nedrick, and Ralph. Now there are two. $4 - 2 = 2$. Nedrick and Ralph were dead.

It had been 6:55 p.m. when the KITTEN Caboodle newspaper came out. It was about 7 p.m. when Alexander had told Ned, "Don't you think someone should be notified?"

At 8 p.m. when the bell tower fell down, Betty, Alexander, and Fred had walked to the other side of the campus. They heard a loud crash but didn't know that the bell tower had fallen over.

They had gone back to Waddle's Doughnuts because of the advertisement that Alexander had seen in the newspaper.

The sign at the counter read:

Alexander asked the man behind the counter,

"Why did you cross out the 'Buy a dozen and get one free' words on your sign?"

"The sale was a great success," the man behind the counter said. "We have been selling zillions of doughnuts. We only have nine doughnuts left so I had to cross off the 'Buy a dozen and get one free' from our sign."

Alexander talked with the doughnut guy for a couple of minutes. They agreed that he would sell Alexander nine doughnuts for the price of eight. Then Alexander would get one doughnut for free.

$$8 + 1 = 9$$

Betty asked, "What are you going to do with nine doughnuts? That's a lot of doughnuts."

"I was going to keep one and give the other eight to you and Fred," Alexander answered.

$$9 - 1 = 8$$

Betty didn't want to get fat on doughnuts and Fred, as everybody knows, is not a big eater. Both Betty and Fred said, "No thank you" at the same time.

It sounded like this: NO THANK YOU.

Betty changed her mind and said, "You keep seven of them, and we'll take two."

$$9 - 7 = 2$$

Your Turn to Play

Here are all the pairs of numbers that add to 9:

$$0 + 9 = 9$$
$$1 + 8 = 9$$
$$2 + 7 = 9$$
$$3 + 6 = 9$$
$$4 + 5 = 9$$

1. In *Life of Fred: Apples*, we did all the numbers that add to 7. Write out a list of all the pairs of numbers that add to 7. Here is a start: $0 + 7 = 7$.

2. If the day after tomorrow is Friday, what day is it today?

3. We know that $4 + 5 = 9$. Then $9 - 5 = ?$

4. If two people say, "No thank you" at the same time it looks like: NO THANK YOU.

What would it look like if three people said "No thank you" at the same time?

·······ANSWERS·······

1. Here are all the pairs of numbers that add to 7:

   $0 + 7 = 7$

   $1 + 6 = 7$

   $2 + 5 = 7$

   $3 + 4 = 7$

2. Sunday

   Monday

   Tuesday

   Wednesday   If the day after tomorrow

   Thursday   is Friday, today must

   Friday   be Wednesday.

   Saturday

3. If $4 + 5 = 9$, then $9 - 5 = 4$.

4. Here is three people saying "No thank you":

   NO THANK YOU.

Chapter Fifteen
Back to His Office

8:05

It was five minutes after 8 and Fred was starting to get sleepy. It had been a long day for a five-year-old.

His eyes were starting to get a little blurry. He knew that it was time to say goodnight to his friends.

Alexander handed one of his nine doughnuts to Betty. They are large doughnuts. In fact, they are huge. That is why they are called Waddles. Betty carried her doughnut using both hands.

When it came to giving Fred his doughnut, Alexander didn't know what to do. Fred's arms couldn't reach around the doughnut.

He set the doughnut on a flat surface.

Fred headed back to his office in the math building. He climbed the stairs to the third floor and headed down the hallway past the vending machines to his office marked "Room 314."

He quietly walked into the room. He didn't want to wake Kingie in case he was asleep.

Fred took the doughnut off of his head and put it down next to his sleeping doll. He knew that Kingie would eat as much of the doughnut as Fred would. In mathematics, 0 = 0.

Normally, Fred would have put the food that he brought home into one of his desk drawers, but this doughnut was too big to fit in a drawer.

Then he noticed a stack of books on the top of his desk that had not been there before. He knew that Kingie had not put them there because Kingie was even shorter than Fred. The only time that Kingie ever was on top of Fred's desk was when Fred put him there.

Fred could read the spines of the books that were on his desk.

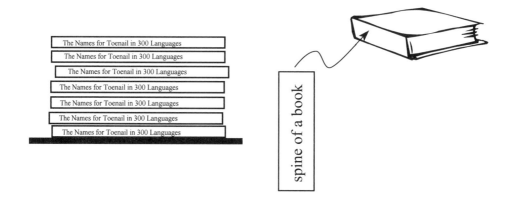

The KITTENS campus mail had done an excellent job of delivering the mail. They didn't just leave the stack of books on the floor in front of Fred's office door. They neatly stacked the books on his desk.

He took one of the copies and put it on a shelf of his library in his office. Since Fred kept his books in alphabetical order . . .

That left six books on Fred's desk. 7 − 1 = 6 When Fred had originally bought the seven copies of the book, he thought of giving *one* copy to Kingie.

Fred changed his mind and decided to give his six extra copies to his doll. Then Kingie could start his own library.

Everyone should have their own library, even if it is just six books.

Fred liked the books in his library. When he had arrived at KITTENS University four years ago, the only thing he owned was his doll. In the beginning his salary was $100 per month. He gave a tenth of that ($10) to Sunday school. The rest ($90) he either saved or spent on books. He spent very little on food or clothing and nothing on housing since he lived for free in his office at the university.

He learned almost everything he knew from books. For example, in the *Naissance of Numeration* book which was right next to *The Names for Toenail in 300 Languages,* Fred learned all about how counting (numeration) first developed (naissance).*

When Nedrick and Ralph were alive, they never learned words like *naissance* because all they did was watch television. Most programs on television use only words that any child can understand.

The ants had already found the doughnut that Fred had put on the floor. They had formed a long line and were taking tiny pieces of the doughnut back to their nest.

Fred lay down on the floor and began to count the ants: 1, 2, 3, 4, 5, 6, 7, 8. . . .

---

* Since *naissance* means a birth or origination of some person, idea, movement, etc., suddenly, for Fred, the word *Renaissance* made sense. The Renaissance was the great rebirth of art and literature that happened from the 1300s to the 1600s in Europe. It is when the medieval world became the modern world.

Three notes:

♪#1: Fred *lay* down on the floor. He didn't *laid*.

Right now, I lie on the couch.

Yesterday, I lay on the couch.

For two days, I have lain on the couch.

In contrast—

Right now, I lay my pencil down.

Yesterday, I laid my pencil down.

Yesterday, my chicken lay down and laid eggs.

♪#2: The numbers 0, 1, 2, 3, 4, 5, . . . are called cardinal numbers. Those are the numbers you use to count things like ants.

Your Turn to Play

1. What is the ordinal number that follows forty-ninth?

2. If you are wondering where the third note is, it will be given in Chapter 16. Copy the previous sentence and circle any cardinal number and underline any ordinal number.

3. 3 + 6 = ?

4. Is *dozen* an ordinal or a cardinal number?

5. {☎} is a set that has the cardinal number 1 associated with it. Name a set that has the cardinal number 2 associated with it.

6. Name a set that has the cardinal number 0 associated with it.

.... **ANSWERS** ....

1. The ordinal number that follows forty-ninth is fiftieth. That is not an easy word to spell. The other way to write fiftieth is 50th.

2. If you are wondering where the <u>third</u> note is, it will be given in Chapter ⑯.

3. $3 + 6 = 9$

4. A dozen is the same as 12. A dozen is a cardinal number. Cardinal numbers are used for counting things. There are a dozen months in a year.

5. Your answer may be different than mine. Here are some sets with the cardinal number 2 associated with them:

   {☎,⌚}

   {my Aunt Hilda, my Aunt Helen}

   {7, 8}

6. Again, your answer may be different than mine.

   The set of all girl scouts who are over 20 feet tall.

   The set of fish that speak German.

   The set of all forks that I have in my pocket.

Or you could simply write { }.

Chapter Sixteen
The Third Note

As Fred lay on the floor watching the ants who were taking away tiny pieces of his doughnut, he counted, ". . . 423, 424, 425, 426. . . ."

After an hour, his numbers were getting larger—877, 878, 879, 880—and the doughnut was getting smaller.

He knew that every set had a cardinal number associated with it. He imagined that there might be ten thousand ants in the math building who were going to enjoy his doughnut.

The cardinal number of the set of stars you can see on a clear night is around 4,000.

Then Fred had a very strange thought. First, he knew that in algebra, the whole numbers are defined as 0, 1, 2, 3, 4, 5, 6. . . .

Second, this is the *set* of whole numbers: {0, 1, 2, 3, 4, 5, 6 . . .}.

Third, since every set has a cardinal number associated with it, Fred wondered what cardinal number could be associated with the set {0, 1, 2, 3, 4, 5, 6 . . .}.

The cardinal number associated with {0, 1, 2, 3, 4, 5, 6 . . .} couldn't be 1,000 since there are more than a thousand members of that set.

It couldn't be a million. 1,000,000

It couldn't be a billion. 1,000,000,000

It couldn't be a trillion. 1 followed by 12 zeros

It couldn't be a quadrillion. 1 followed by 15 zeros

It couldn't be a quintillion. 1 followed by 18 zeros

This takes us to our third note.

♪#3: The last of the arithmetic books is *Life of Fred: Decimals and Percents.*

After that comes:

Life of Fred: Pre-Algebra 1

Life of Fred: Pre-Algebra 2

Life of Fred: Beginning Algebra

Life of Fred: Advanced Algebra

Life of Fred: Geometry

Life of Fred: Trig

and then two years of college calculus *Life of Fred: Calculus.*

In one of the courses after trig, we begin the arithmetic of the numbers beyond 0, 1, 2, 3, 4, 5, 6, 7, 8, 9,10, 11. . . .

You will be told the cardinal number associated with {0, 1, 2, 3, 4, 5, 6 . . .}. Since you don't want to wait all those years to find out the answer, here it is now. The cardinal number associated with the set of all whole numbers is aleph-null. It is written as $\aleph_0$. The letter $\aleph$ is the first letter of the Hebrew alphabet.

Now you know how many whole numbers there are.

Aleph-null is an infinite number. It is the smallest infinite number. When you get older, we will tell you about a bigger infinite number which is called $\aleph_1$.

And then, of course, $\aleph_2, \aleph_3, \aleph_4 \ldots$.

Do you think we stop there? Mathematicians like to play. They find a number bigger than any of these alephs.

Meanwhile . . . Fred is counting the ants: 2,004, 2,005, 2,006—and he was starting to feel sleepy. He got up and headed down the hallway to the restroom where he kept his bathroom stuff.

He flossed his teeth.

He brushed his teeth.

He rinsed his mouth.

He looked in the mirror and wondered what he might look like if he had a moustache when he grew up.

He headed back to his office. The doughnut was almost all gone.

The ants were very happy.

He unrolled his three-foot long sleeping bag and put it under his desk.

Then he looked at the books on the walls of his office. He often liked to pick out a book to read before he headed off to sleep at night.

He took *Alice's Adventures in Wonderland* off the shelf and opened it. It is a fun book, but Fred wasn't in the mood for crazy tea parties tonight.

He thought about reading *Moby Dick* again. When Fred was younger, he had read this sea story about a nutty captain going after the great white whale called Moby Dick.

Last year he had read *Don Quixote* (pronounced kee-HOE-tee). It was about this crazy guy who thought he was a knight and went around doing all the things he thought knights did. The only problem was that the time of knights was hundreds of years before Quixote.

Only last week Fred learned something that shocked him: On the deeper level, *Alice* had nothing to do with tea parties! *Moby* had nothing to do with whale hunting! *Quixote* had nothing to do with being a knight!

For adult readers, Moby Dick is much more than just a big whale.*

Your Turn to Play

1. This has been a tough chapter. Let's start off with something easy: $6 + 3 = ?$

2. The whole numbers $\{0, 1, 2, 3, 4 \ldots\}$ are infinite. They never stop. There is always a bigger number. If someone tells you that a trillion (1,000,000,000,000) is the largest number, you can say, "a trillion, one." (1,000,000,000,001). Name a number bigger than a quintillion. (That is 1 followed by 18 zeros.)

3. $7 + 2 = ?$

4. How many ears are on these rabbits?

---

* Moby Dick can represent, for example, the malignancy of oppressive feelings of self-alienation that can only be exorcised by engaging in self-destructive acts.

. . . . ANSWERS . . . .

1. $6 + 3 = 9$

2. Your answer may be different than mine. Here are some numbers that are bigger than a quintillion:

     A quintillion, one

     1,000,000,000,000,000,001

     Two quintillion

     A googol, which is 1 followed by a hundred zeros

3. $7 + 2 = 9$

4. The easiest way to count those ears is to count by twos.

    2   4   6   8   10   12

Chapter Seventeen
Nighttime Reading

Fred decided to read a book about Donald Duck! That has to be a real surprise. For someone who has read and enjoyed books like *Moby Dick* and *Don Quixote*, it must seem weird that Fred would choose such a simple book ... except that this book was in German.

eine Ente = a duck

Fred couldn't think of a nicer way to learn German.

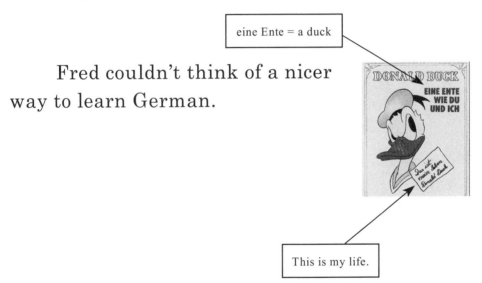

This is my life.

He sat on top of his sleeping bag and started reading.

He opened the book up to Chapter 1 (Kapitel 1) and read: Most baby ducks want to slip out of their eggs as fast as possible. (Die meisten Entenküken schlüpfen so schnell wie möglich aus dem Ei heraus.)

Donald didn't seem to be in a hurry to come out of his egg. His mother yelled at him: Come out of there right now, Donald! (Jetzt komm endlich heraus, Donald!)

Fred giggled. That woke up Kingie who came and sat on Fred's lap. Kingie liked to be read to. It didn't matter to him if it was in English or German. Dolls understand every language.

After Fred had finished reading, Kingie had a question. He asked about the six copies of *The Names for Toenail in 300 Languages* that Fred had put next to him while he was sleeping.

Fred explained that that was a gift for him.

Kingie thanked Fred. Then he thought of sharing some of his copies with others. Fred told him that Betty and Alexander already had copies of the book.

"That's not a problem," Kingie said. "I'll keep a copy and send the other five to my brothers." $6 - 1 = 5$.

"Your brothers!" Fred exclaimed. "I didn't know you had brothers."

Kingie explained, "When the man at King of French Fries gave me to you, I had five brothers that he gave to other kids."

Kingie put one copy of the book next to his art supplies and wrapped up the other five copies for mailing.

He addressed the packages:

Kenneth
Wichita, Kansas

Kendric
Topeka, Kansas

Karney
Dodge City, Kansas

Kermit
Salina, Kansas

Kory
Concordia, Kansas

"All your brothers live in Kansas," Fred noticed.

"I have other brothers," Kingie explained. "For example, Gael, Gallagher, Galvin, Garrett, and Gilroy all live in Georgia."

Fred was starting to see a pattern. He asked Kingie about brothers in Kentucky, and Kingie said that they also had names starting with K.

Kingie asked Fred to mail the packages. It was difficult for Kingie to walk long distances.

Kingie

Fred was happy to do that for his doll. Kingie told Fred to remember to put on a coat since in Kansas it gets cold at 8:20 on a February evening.

Over his pajamas, he put on a shirt, pants, mittens, scarf, coat, ear muffs, and a hat. He put on his biggest boots (size 2). He gave Kingie a hug, picked up the five packages, and headed out the door.

Then down the hallway past the nine vending machines—five on one side and four on the other.

Just as he was about to head down the stairs he realized that there was a campus mailbox right next to the vending machines. He put Kingie's packages in the box and the special light on the top of the box turned on.

As he stood there, two things happened.

an ordinal number

First, a student letter carrier rushed over to the box and took out Kingie's five packages.

a cardinal number

Second, Fred started to feel very warm. He was standing in the hallway of the math building where it was 65°. Fred was dressed for ten degrees below zero (−10°).

hot Fred

Your Turn to Play

1. When Fred asked Kingie about his brothers in Kentucky, he had thought about two states that started with the same letter. (Kentucky and Kansas)

Then he thought about the set of states beginning with M: {Maine, Maryland, Massachusetts, Michigan, Minnesota, Mississippi, Missouri, Montana}. What is the cardinal number of that set?

2. That was a lot of states starting with M. But there is another set of states starting with a different letter that also has eight members. What letter is that?

3. 5 + 2 = ?

4. 5 + 4 = ?

5. (hard question) There is only one state in the United States that begins with R. Kingie's brother Ryan lives in that state. What state is that?

6. 9 − 6 = ?

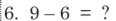

······ANSWERS·······

1. The cardinal number of {Maine, Maryland, Massachusetts, Michigan, Minnesota, Mississippi, Missouri, Montana} is 8.

2. There are also eight states that begin with the letter N: Nebraska, Nevada, New Hampshire, New Jersey, New Mexico, New York, North Carolina, and North Dakota.

3. $5 + 2 = 7$

4. $5 + 4 = 9$

5.    This is a map of Rhode Island.

6. $9 - 6 = 3$

A small note about infinity

A set is infinite if you could never finish counting the members. The set goes on forever like the years you will spend in Heaven.

There are lots of infinite sets. For example:

The natural numbers {1, 2, 3, 4, . . .}
The whole numbers {0, 1, 2, 3, . . .}
The integers { . . . −3, −2, −1, 0, 1, 2, 3, . . .}

The symbol used for *any* infinite set is ∞. But ∞ is not a number. It just means infinite.

The *number* of natural numbers is $\aleph_0$.

The *number* of points on a line is $\aleph_1$.

In later math, we will show you why all these things are true.

Chapter Eighteen
Letters from Brothers

Fred wanted to play. He took off his hat and put a sticky note on it that read: "To Fred Gauss, room 314, math building." Then he put it in the mailbox.

The light on the top of the box went on. Then he ran like crazy down the hallway to his office. In the language of running, he *sprinted*.

He opened his office door and on his desk was . . .

Campus mail at KITTENS University is fast.

Fred took off his ear muffs, boots, coat, scarf, mittens, pants, and shirt. In his pajamas he felt just right—not too hot and not too cold.

Kingie was busy reading five letters that he had received from Kenneth, Kendric, Karney, Kermit and Kory.

Here is Kenneth's letter:

Wichita, Kansas
February

Dear Brother Kingie,
    Thank you for the beautiful book you
sent to me this evening. I always wanted to
know the names for toenail.
                    You are in my prayers,
                    Ken

Kenneth, Kendric, Karney, Kermit and
Kory all knew that you should always thank
someone for gifts they give to you.

When Fred read to Kingie, Kingie always
remembered to thank Fred.

If someone is reading this book to you, give
them a kiss, a hug, or shake their hand and tell
them, "Thank you."

Fred wanted to play with Kingie before they
headed to bed. Fred suggested they play tea
party. One of them could pretend to pour the tea
and ask how many lumps of sugar the other one
wanted.

Kingie shook his head. He said he wanted real American food. He wanted pizza.

"American food?" Fred asked. "That's silly."

Fred explained:

---

1. Five hundred (500) years before Christ, the soldiers of King Darius baked bread on their shields and added cheese and dates.

2. In the hundred years before Christ, Virgil wrote one of the world's most famous poems, the *Aeneid*. (pronounced eh-KNEE-id).

One line reads: "See, we devour the plates on which we fed." Those plates were made of flour.

3. In 997 A.D. pizza appeared in Medieval Latin.

4. People who came from Italy in the late 1800s were the first to introduce pizza to the United States.

"So," Fred continued, "it would be silly to call it an American food."

Kingie was convinced . . . but he still wanted pizza. Fred grabbed a whole bunch of nickels he had in his desk and headed down the hallway to the vending machines.

The small pizza was a dollar ($1.00), which is a hundred cents (100¢). Fred put in his nickels and counted by fives: 5, 10, 15, 20, 25, 30, 35, 40, 45, 50, 55, 60, 65, 70, 75, 80, 85, 90, 95, 100. Out popped a hot pizza.

It was too hot for him to carry in his bare hands. He noticed that the campus mail box was right next to the pizza vending machine.

With his finger he wrote in the melted cheese Room 314 and then slid the pizza into the mail box.

The light on the top of the box went on.

Fred sprinted back to his office.

Your Turn to Play

1. Count by fives from 120 to 160. It will begin with 120, 125. . . .

2. It was getting late.
What time was it?

3. What is the next number after 60?

4. What is the next number after
four million? (4,000,000)

5. How many feet are there in a yard? (Hint: it is one smaller than four.) Fred is one yard tall.

6. What is the ordinal number that comes right after seventh?

7. What is the cardinal number that comes right after 82?

.... ANSWERS ....

1. 120, 125, 130, 135, 140, 145, 150, 155, 160

2. It is 8:30.

Some people say that it
is "half past eight."

3. The next number after 60 is 61.

4. The next number after four million is four million
one. This can also be written as 4,000,001.

5. There are three feet in a yard.

6. The ordinal number than comes right after seventh
is eighth. This can also be written as 8th.

7. The cardinal number that comes right after 82 is 83.

Chapter Nineteen
Mysteries of Life

Fred could never figure out how campus mail did it. Did they fax it? Did they use airplanes? There are many things in life that remain mysteries.

But there it was . . .

. . . a hot pizza waiting there for him and for Kingie.

Fred put Kingie on the desktop. Kingie wasted no time. He started eating. He told Fred that being an artist is hard work, and he was hungry.

Fred wanted to wait a while until the pizza had cooled off before he began eating. He got placemats, napkins, knives, forks, plates, and cups out of a desk drawer.

He put the placemat down first. Then the plate and napkin.

Then the fork on top of the napkin. Knife and spoon on the right with the knife next to the plate. The cup above the knife.

Meanwhile, Kingie was standing in the middle of the pizza and eating.

Fred looked in his desk drawers for some hot chocolate mix. He couldn't find any. When he looked up, he saw that Kingie had finished the pizza.

Fred thought: *I really wasn't very hungry actually.* Why Fred never gets around to eating is another one of the mysteries of life.

After Fred cleaned up, the pair of them snuggled into Fred's sleeping bag. Fred didn't have to brush his teeth again, because he hadn't eaten.

Kingie smelled like pizza.

With the light out, they could see Orion through the window.

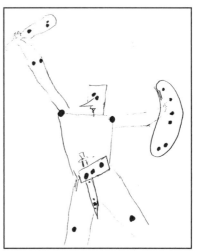

Fred said his prayers. It had been a wonderful Monday. They fell asleep.

I f you would like a bit of practice with the addition and subtraction that you have learned so far, here is your chance.

First, get a blank piece of paper and a pencil.

On the next page of this book put the left edge of your paper over the wavy lines to cover the answer.

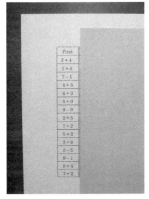

Write your answers on your blank sheet of paper.

After you have finished a column, check your answers.

First		Second		Third	
3 + 4	7	2 + 5	7	6 + 1	7
1 + 6	7	4 + 3	7	5 + 2	7
7 − 1	6	7 − 3	4	7 − 2	5
4 + 5	9	5 + 4	9	3 + 6	9
6 + 3	9	7 + 2	9	2 + 7	9
5 + 0	5	3 + 0	3	88 + 0	88
9 − 9	0	7 − 7	0	33 − 33	0
2 + 5	7	1 + 6	7	6 + 1	7
7 + 2	9	6 + 3	9	2 + 7	9
5 + 2	7	5 + 2	7	2 + 2	4
3 + 6	9	3 + 4	7	2 + 5	7
5 − 5	0	27 − 27	0	12 − 1	11
9 − 1	8	6 − 1	5	10 − 1	9
0 + 4	4	0 + 32	32	1 + 3	4
7 + 2	9	8 + 1	9	1 + 9	10

Index

126

If you would like to learn more about books written about Fred . . .

FredGauss.com

Gauss is Fred's last name.
It rhymes with house.